Wedding Day

DANA LEVIN

Wedding Day

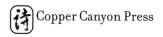 Copper Canyon Press

Cover art: *Me and My Human*, photo, Vincent Laforet / The New York Times

Copper Canyon Press is in residence at Fort Worden State Park in Port Townsend, Washington, under the auspices of Centrum Foundation. Centrum is a gathering place for artists and creative thinkers from around the world, students of all ages and backgrounds, and audiences seeking extraordinary cultural enrichment.

LIBRARY OF CONGRESS CATALOGING-IN-PUBLICATION DATA

Levin, Dana.
Wedding day / Dana Levin.
   p. cm.
Includes bibliographical references.
ISBN 1-55659-219-1 (pbk.: alk. paper)
1. Title.
PS3562.E88953W43 2005
811'.54—DC22   2004017702

9 8 7 6 5 4 3 2

First Printing

COPPER CANYON PRESS
Post Office Box 271
Port Townsend, Washington 98368
www.coppercanyonpress.org

ACKNOWLEDGMENTS

Thanks to the editors of the following publications, in which these poems first appeared (sometimes in different forms and under different titles):

The Alembic: "Desire (flesh field)"

American Poetry Review: "Ars Poetica (cocoons)," "Ars Poetica (the idea)," "Ars Poetica (pollen)," "Working Methods," "Adept"

The Atlantic Monthly: "It Was Yoked to a Black Hunger"

Colorado Review: "Sumer Is Icumen In"

Conduit: "Gift Drawing,""I Hunched Boiling Inside It"

Countermeasures: "Quelquechose," "White Field," "Painting Vacation"

Forklift: "White Dog"

Gulf Coast: "Cinema Verité"

The Kenyon Review: "Techno," "Suttee," "The Washing"

Luna: "American Poet"

Ploughshares: "Desire (clear place)"

Poetry: "Above the Neck"

Pool: "Isolato"

Pushcart Prize XXVIII: Best of the Small Presses, Pushcart Press, 2004: "Adept"

Pushcart Prize XXIX: Best of the Small Presses, Pushcart Press, 2005: "Quelquechose"

Rivendell: "Glory," "Quelquechose" (reprint)

Third Coast: "Desire (golden mean)"

This Art: Poems about Poetry, Copper Canyon Press, 2003: "Ars Poetica (cocoons)," "Ars Poetica (pollen)"

VOLT: "I Asked Why I Was Better at Truth than Love"

Washington Square: "Glass Heart," "Ambivalent Light"

For their presence and encouragement: my sisters Laura Terris and Caryn McCloskey; Shari Lee, Sebastian Matthews, Jeanie Tietjen—as well as for their time and insight: Jon Davis, Matt Donovan, Greg Glazner, Jennifer Levin, Gretchen Mattox, Carol Moldaw, Malena Mörling, Barry Sanders, Sam Hamill and Michael Wiegers, and especially, Dan George and Louise Glück.

Much gratitude to the College of Santa Fe, the Lannan Foundation's Marfa Residency Program, the Mendocino Arts Center, and the National Endowment for the Arts for supporting this book's conception and completion.

Contents

Wedding Day

The outer sun hungers for the inner one.

JACOB BÖEHME, *De Signatura Rerum*

ONE

Techno

I was tracking the stars through the open truck window,
      my friend speeding the roads through the black country —

and I was thinking how the songs coming from the radio
      were like the speech of a single human American psyche —

the one voice of the one collective dream, industrial, amphetamine,
      and the stars unmoving —

the countryside black and silent, through which a song pumped *serious killer*
      over and over —

and I could feel the nation shaping, it was something about the collective
      dream of the rich land and the violent wanting —

the amphetamine drive and the cows sleeping, all along the sides
      of the dark road —

never slowing enough to see what we might have seen if the moon rose up
      its pharmaceutical light —

aspirin-blue over the pine-black hills what was rising up —

mullein or something else in the ditches their flameless tapers —

world without fire the song heralded a crystal methedrine light —

while the sky brought its black bone down around the hood of the truck
      the electronic migration —

we were losing our bodies—

digitized salt of bytes and speed we were becoming a powder—

light—

bicarbonate—

what we might have seen, if we had looked—

Cinema Verité

And the lights go down—
hush.

And a light comes up—
the screen.

That brightens, so well, our dark day.
That brightens

to a fountain in a square,
dolphins without their tails—
without their heads.
Just their arched backs
crowning a chaos of broken nymphs, what's left
of the government
of the sea—
The light shifts.
Widens.
Black-and-white

necklace of fires
erupting from the gas line, buildings bereft
of facades—

strangers picking through a desolation, passports,
lovers,
gone—

then weeping in French.
Then credits in French in Czech in Deutsch then

the Village cafés, *joie*
to the nth
degree —

trumpeting out, like loud flowers,
along Bleecker Street.

After which there's a drink.

Then a toke, beside the garbage cans —

And then a late train and a key in the lock and the lights going up
in the den of the metropolitan
twelve o'clock
with its last
hopeful seconds, that we won't
go to bed bored —

Hush.

Thoughts everywhere taxiing hurriedly.

A little like New York, isn't it,
ceaseless hive, humming despite a historical
exhaustion — Outside

the sky's
apartment panorama. Every twelfth window blued
with light —

beacons of the bag-eyed tribe called
Who Bricked the Doorway to Sleep—

    3 AM, slumped on the couch, to surf
the blood
    and promise:

    dances to banish the hunch 'n' shiver
the Claritin the Klonopin new
    kind of soap for an old kind of stain, channels
surging toward the sea—

Wire of light.

    Dawn sheen
thin along the river.

    Burrowing
into every screen in your single room
    like an IV,
feeding the face that will medicate
    the blood in the day,
anchor
    tethering you
to *news*—

    until you step out
into the afternoon glare,
    snap on the dark lenses,
foam of gray speakers into your ears and pump up

a perfect noise
to soundtrack the filmed-over day—

thinking, What time does it start.

thinking, I am so late.

thinking, Not the 6 but the B, the B to the N, the N
to the light
   flooding the stairs up to Union Square and opening out
onto a kind of joy, the escape into the art
   of another country's pain,
and then the screen fades and the people stand and the bright suffering
   comes to an end—

No.

Yes.

How.

Ars Poetica

Six monarch butterfly cocoons
      clinging to the back of your throat —

      you could feel their gold wings trembling.

You were alarmed. You felt infested.
In the downstairs bathroom of the family home,
      gagging to spit them out —
              and a voice saying, *Don't, don't* —

Glass Heart

could the West creep in to your idea of happiness — abundance
      which gave no comfort,
                  in which your loneliness was spared —

~

The student wrote: she wipes tears from her heart.

   Forgotten, on the kitchen table — glassy, beaded with sweat —

The line is too sentimental, said the teacher, unless I see it literally: taking
a sponge to the anatomical heart, wiping and wiping the tears off it —

   glass heart, so transparent — the tears drove around its autobahn

   Then the kids came home and found it pulsing there. Like in a
   washing machine, you could see the grief go round and round —

The student wrote: sucking tears out of her aorta with a straw —

   a bitterness so pronounced it was a kind of ammonia, a world
   in which one could lose one's parents and be put on a train alone —

   Her grandfather had owned a little store for years. They can shoot
   out the windows, he would say, wagging a finger, as long as they
   don't set the street on fire —

glass heart, so transparent

Was it their mother's, their father's? It lay weeping in the heat.
But they had to leave, to help deliver groceries —

The student wrote: in my left my heart my right my bone, beating my heart
like a bloody drum —

Ovens, the grandfather muttered. In Russia they ate us raw.

so transparent

Meal after meal no one claimed it. After a while no one saw it,
though it ticked at the center of the table like a clock —

singing O, this sack of water, swaying on its hook of bone.

Ars Poetica

would it wake the drowned out of their anviled sleep —

would it slip the sun like a coin behind their eyes —

The idea, the teacher said, was that there was a chaos
left in matter — a little bit of not-yet in everything that was —

so the poets became interested in fragments, interruptions —
the little bit of saying lit by the unsaid —

was it a way to stay alive, a way to keep hope,
leaving things unfinished?

as if in completing a sentence there was death —

Quelquechose

You want to get in and then get out of the box.

form breakage form

I was in the fish shop, wondering why being experimental means
      not having a point—

      why experimentation in form is sufficient unto itself
          (is it?)—

But I needed a new way to say things: sad tired *I*
      with its dulled violations, lyric with loss in its faculty den—

Others were just throwing a veil over suffering:
      glittery interesting I-don't-exist—

All over town, I marched around,
      ranting my jeremiad.

Thinking, What good is form if it doesn't *say anything*—

And by "say" I meant "wake somebody up."

Even here at the shores of Lake Champlain
      mothers were wrenching small arms out of sockets.

Not just the mothers. What were the fathers doing,
        wrenching small arms out of bedside caches —

How could I disappear into language when children were being called
        "fuckers" —
                by their mothers —

        who were being called "cunts" by their boyfriends —

        who were being called "dickheads" behind their backs —

It wasn't that I was a liberal democrat, it was that
                bodies had been divested of their souls —

        like poems —

Trying to get in or out of the box.

And the scallops said, *"Nulles idées que dans les choses."*

And I said, "I'll have the Captain's Special with wedges instead of fries."

And everywhere in the fish shop the argument raged, its baroque
        proportions, the conflict between harmony and invention.

But then a brilliance —

The movement of her gloved hands as she laid the haddock out
        one by one —

The sheered transparency of her latexed fingers,
        in and out of the lit display case as if they were yes, fish —

Laying haddock out in a plastic tub on a bed of ice,
      her lank brown hair pulled back from her face with a band—

Yes it was true she had to do this for the market
      but there was such beauty in it—

      she was the idea called Tenderness—

      she was a girl who stood under fluorescent lights making
            six bucks an hour—

      and she looked up at me and held out a haddock with both her hands,
            saying it was the best of the morning's catch.

Ars Poetica

this hush, my pollen — the ordinary grace in the buds,
    the crowding,
        my basement sorrows — salt and shadow, saying
        Lucky, lucky, your tiniest sadness,
this desert of fragments,
        openhanded voyage,
           this urge to making a scrapbook of stars —

American Poet

For weeks every Friday I went to see films at the School of Theology.

Every Friday I would get there half an hour early so I could buy candy
      at the store that closed at seven.

I would walk out around the building and lean against a wall
      facing Foothill Boulevard,
watching the blood and pearl of cars as they sped in opposite directions.

And every Friday there would be a cricket trilling endlessly
      against the din of traffic.

Inaudible, unless you stood right at the spot where it lodged itself
      in the little crack between the walk and the wall—

It legged the air ceaselessly where no one could hear it.

I would stand right next to it and watch the traffic stream.

Thinking it was like an American poet.

The moon pooled. The cars wheeled and wheeled.

Glory

The terrible aesthetics of the red and blue in the pasteled yards,
    against the soft pink of camellias.

An affront to beauty in a purely visual sense.

Purely, that white assertion, when nothing was *purely* anymore —

The flags, and the violets in regiment below them.

The dandelions in chaos below them —

The river of rage and peace that is a river of bones.

The river of flame and peace that is a river of ash —

The story of guns in someone else's city, every day with your toast
    and coffee —

Then the red and blue over the green of the park, oranged
    in the trash can fires.

Could anything be purely aesthetic

when appearance was the symptom of a disease —

You drove past them under a regiment of stars.

Over the terran order.

It was a holiday but you needed to work, debt rising around you
  like a flood.

～

And would the guns and the city ever wake each other up,
would they wake each other, if they stood at a juncture —

Through the underpasses. Each break in the broadcast
an eye closing, a hand sliding over a face.

～

The river of pain and the river of willed forgetfulness.

The river of blood and the river of powders crushed —

The terrible aesthetics of the red and blue over the chemical fields,
  the milk-green vats in the sun —

The aesthetics of not knowing what was inside them, of the vermilion
  sunset right now.

The river of heat and the river of ice in our drinks.

The river of heat through the sluice of your throat, the ignition
  you won't turn on —

still you couldn't make it mean

when nothing was *purely* anymore.

The river of heat and the muzzle at the river of veins.

The aesthetics of not knowing what was inside you,
    behind the green vats lighting in the night —

You thought you were alone as we swam the channels of distraction.

But traffic flowed like plasma: Purity going one way, Sacrifice
    another —

Suttee

Cars oiling slowly through the rich grid of the Basin.

White, red, the chaining hemoglobes, from the ridge
    you watched them,
their *shhh* and *wahhh*
    wafting up through the canyon,
the medicine-smelling trees —

Eucalyptus.

Pink stars of ice plant, night-drained of color.

Open your mouth, he said.

Do you want Batman or Spider-Man.

Do you want the wizard hat or Professor X, the green skull
    with a rose in its teeth, do you want

the thunderbolt or the smiley face.

George Washington with spirals for eyes.

You were a feelingless light —

without parents or hunger —

sliding your back along the length of the car,
        then slipping to the glass-smacked ground —

and found the moon analgesic —

pocked and chemical for your
        amputated tongue,
you opened your mouth and he steadied your head,
        and slipped another president in —

and walked you
        to the cement-lined river, furious
for the mercury-ridden sea —

after days of hard rain, palm fronds smashed up
        against the overpass pilings, shopping cart
streaming by —

saying, Do you want Aquaman or the Sacred Heart.
        That elephant god, Remover
of Obstacles,
        Mary with her methadone eyes.

                    ⌒

You followed the rush.

Swift as vapor together you skimmed
        along that chocolate vein, there was a glow

at the end
      of the water—

Was it the sea
      opening and closing its phosphorous hand,
there was a fist in your chest
      that kept mimicking it,
it was flesh-encrusted, it needed to be
      phosphored clean—

Smoke. Smell of gasoline.
      And then you saw it, something shipwrecked
against an overpass rail, burning cocoon
      of flame—

You didn't move. You didn't think about a driver—
      You stood starry as its image
trembled in the water
      like a butterfly trapped in oil—

and took his hand. Ravishing,
      the hot chemistry.
You walked toward the burning machine.

It Was Yoked to a Black Hunger

The raven lifted.
Circled like a skate on a groove of air—

the fur at the neck ruffled up.

Ruffling up,
each follicle trying
to leave that meat
as the raven swooped down, poked its beak
into that beating snuff,
the rabbit not dead not yet—

it pecked and pecked, until the one red spot welled up.

A thin steam from the rabbit, like a wick blown out.

The snow sparkling.

And the raven cocked its black eye, dipped its beak
in the red pool
it had made—

for the ink of elegy.

Wh▮▮ield

over which you hover with a flaming glass —
        saying,

There is a fire in it,
        an invisible burning left in nature that demands to be revealed —

        ⌒‿⌒

And as I was coming around the trail a hummingbird perched
on a thin top branch and it was a sign to me: hummingbird,
green emblem of joy —

Then a black-spotted butterfly with orange wings in the yellow
chamisa — it was a sign of my transformation —

        ignoring the grand indifference, the way the pines
                took no notice of you
        as they dropped their cones,
                needled branches swaying in a conspiracy of wind —

        ⌒‿⌒

When the man emerged from the brush with a knife

        was that the kind of burning you meant?

When the man emerged —

It was the way the sun came through the cottonwood leaves and coined
them up into gold disks slight fire at the edges a whole treasure of them in
a half-moon carpet on the east side of the tree it was the way the leaves
split light into scales that put me on the mountain sugared with pollen and
the pox of violence the way the sun flamed up into strings the few red
strands of his hair the bronze the burning creation all the arson inside

> *that could give you a fire*
> > *out of which to speak, give you a fire*
> *in which to wait out the terror,*
> > *if a man emerged from the brush with a knife,*
> > > *scattering the gravel with his feet —*

⌒‿

And when I wrote *the sun lifted* — Each aspen went up like a torch —

Little *l*, thin as a match — Turning the word into the world —

> *where the chamisa smelled like honey — even a yellow dust of it*
> > *on his forehead*
> *as he advanced, where you stood mute —*
> > *spores so thick they*
> *closed the throat, where you read it —*
> > *past all*
> *paralysis to understand the sign: it was*
> > *nobody's sweetness —*
> *as he came crouching forward, knife drawn,*
> > > *into the white, white field —*

The Washing

Everyone's got their massacre site just around the corner.
JIM LANDALE, HAGUE SPOKESMAN, KOSOVO

I

In the mirror, open your mouth.
Press down on your tongue and say Ahh.
Ah. Red-tipped,
       against the black back reaches of the throat —

Reflected Self, dip in.
Reach out from the mirror and dip in.
Dip in to the open mouth.
Dip in your fingers and climb in.

So that you stand in the middle of your throat —
in the ribbed-slick cavern of the throat —
so that you stand

at a pool — saying

Ah, Ah, Ach, Ich, the red leaf of the willow trailing
      like hair
over the black
      water.

Get down on your knees and look in.
Bring yourself close and look in.
A's and B's, upglistening like fish.
Upglistening and then lifting
      over the pool,
Ahh, Behh, breath over water in the air around you,

31

what will you bathe, Throat-Stander,
      in the song's black pool?

    II

Foot bones gleaming whitely in a scrim of dew:
      sigh now, so beautiful.

The war is over, *so*
      beautiful —

Like they're hunting for mushrooms, the pathologists crouch
      in their paper suits
around the lip of an open hole —

each body a bagged tuber
      dug up from the ground, roots
with a little meat on them —

and then they see it,
      beyond the dandelions edging their
paper shoes,
      and turn their masked faces,
bend to the foot with their latexed hands,
      touching but not feeling,
looking but not
      breathing it in —

      it is evidence, it is not
to be eaten —

      it is evidence of the world's
game of shards,

how will they syntax
the fragments —

perched like a bulb in one rubbered hand,
if they plant it
    will a whole man grow?

Sigh now, the war over, so beautiful.

III

And you say, Oh lighten up.

Lighten up, you say, the sun's
    on your back, lighten up —

I lightened —

I lightened when my neighbor's ax came down.

Drifted up with the smoke
    roiling out from my house — it looked
like a loaf on fire.

And the reporter said,
    They walked away singing.

Said, Finished them
    with shots to the head.

Said, Foot and pool, *f* and *t*, *p* and *l* —

IV

Reach out from the mirror, dip in.
Into the open mouth, dip in.
Dip in your fingers and climb in.

So that you crouch at the pool in the middle
        of your throat, the dark,
the alphabetic
        pool—

and watch the sounds uplift like steam,
        the shape of *ah*
sighing out the portal of your open mouth
        and spreading

over the mirror's glass field,
        staining it
to prove that you're alive—

We will bathe it here, lovingly.

Lave, lave, the word *laver*, washing over it like a mother's
        hand—

We will take the foot
        and dip it in the worded water.

TWO

Working Methods

I was falling asleep, wondering how to describe the poet's studio, when a
voice said, "You have to be your own absence, with fifty percent deity."

woke up with: *I false — into arrangement; am out of it — deranged —*
woke up with: *hurry up is flamboyant and resolutional —*
woke up with: *as the ask progresses to a tiny new yes —*

My friend Dan says: Listen — Record — Orchestrate.

PLAYING

I was telling Dan that sometimes I get directions or lines for a poem by
doodling — like how *"Isolato with a crown... / Isolato with a barge"* came from
writing the word ISOLATO and putting a box around it and doodling
around the box until one edge of it elongated into a tall thing wearing a
crown-looking thing and the whole box looked like that thing on a barge.

He wanted to try it, so I said, "Give me a word." And he said, "Jang Kwon."
And I said, "What's that?" And he said, "Heel-palm." And I knew it was a
kung fu move — so I wrote JANG KWON and put a box around it and we
each started doodling and writing commentary on each other's doodling
and on each other's commentary and did some cutting and here is
the poem:

JANG KWON (HEEL-PALM)

Like a tack, thunder defines the cloud.

Hand splaying, the fletching of an arrow

But the technique was not an arrow,
         hand or foot —

Was not an asking of what was next — :

The bent cherry
         shedding light above the flat and empty ground.

WATCHING

When the poem begins, a curtain draws back. There is a stage for the mind's
Moulin Rouge —

where the image gets its aria —

Pull the curtain: severed foot in a daisied green.
Pull the curtain: anatomical heart: a fortified city.
In the Panopticon, a throat in flames —

The eye swoops back, swoops in.

MAKING

Dream: *A test for my beginning poetry workshop: on a page is the barest outline of
a fish and the instructions say, "Now draw a more serious fish."*

Dream: *A poem hangs in the air like a curtain. It dismantles itself until all that
remains are single words. They shimmer: nouns and verbs.*

You must be your own absence, with fifty percent deity.
You must ask, Why this song, this seeing.

THREE

I Asked Why I Was Better at Truth than Love

Keyhole.
     Stick your finger in.
You can open it now, enter the room made
     completely of light —
You can stand there now.
     See
the womb unattached to any body, floating
     in the aseptic white
like a weightless dark balloon —
     And there, a little lit bean,
pulsing weakly inside it.
     And a choir is singing.
At each corner of the ceiling, thousands shunted
     next to one another,
stiff as little pins —
     Singing *O trunk of glass, O open eye*
and the little bean opens its eyes.
     Grows child-sized.
And the nubs come out, on tendrils from either side of its spine.
     You ask,
Will it have a heart?
     And the carbon in its chest
flames up in a vise, diamond in a pool
     of fire —
And the womb vanishes.
     It stands white and tall before you,
moving the air.
     You ask,
What about the father?
     And it lifts its voice with the choir singing

O brilliancy and cold —
>And you ask,

What about the mother?

>And it looks into you with eyes of ice, which it will never close,

not even in sleep,

>and suddenly you're in the hospital nursery, looking down at yourself

inside the glass box

>trying to turn away

from the fluorescents constant everywhere around you

>and the angel comes to your ear like a wind, says Mother?

There wasn't a mother.

>There was light.

Ambivalent Light

The sperm swam fast and straight through its collapsing brothers,
      the mucus layers parting like veils —

I was telling Doctor C. about the dream of throwing the ashtray at my
mother and feeling the ashes inside it and he said "The ashes inside?"
and I thought how the ashtray had been oddly shaped, almost like a womb,
and I said "I was throwing her womb back at her," and I was delighted—

YOU ARE A POCKET

the soul, shaped like an aspirin

FOR SOME KIND OF LIGHT

"Least of all was she a 'thing'; she was intensely, fearfully, a person—"

As a child she particularly enjoyed looking at the pictures painted by
mental patients in the Time-Life book *The Mind.*

Her favorite page was the one with the inside of a head, where all sorts of
terrible things were transpiring in different compartments of the brain.

The crow strapped to the hospital gurney, flailing on its back, as masked
doctors advanced with needles and knives—

Excuse me for coming here again and again.

For not knowing how to make it new.

For not knowing
                how to freshen it up,

this old game, *Suffering*:

Red worm called I breathe I suck,
        mother in seclusion, sisters
regulated
        away—

And then I was human,
        in a box, in a room, white nurses hovering and zipping away
like white bees,
        silver and busy—making sure I stayed

sensate and feeling—
        making sure I endured

Thought and Wanting—
        when the bodiless world was cool and light
and forms stayed
        in their glimmery thin perfections—

I wanted to get published, I wanted to get married,
gather those fruits up
        in my bandaged hands, breathe them deeply in,
brace of iron around my chest, how
        could I have hoped to hold those things
when I didn't know
        if I wanted
a body—

Above the Neck

Little winks from the tips of silvered tools —

you sat in stars.

Garaged dark.

And a skein of bandages on a little stool.

Wrapped you up, my   mental pupa —

On a metal folding chair.

And all around you synapses
        pop and flare —

I'd been taking the walk called
        Head Bobbing on a Font of Blood —

I couldn't believe I had legs

as the ditch streamed by —

spider-egged in a web of squares: chair, house, mind...

Iron-press of your mummy-suit.

Head free
        to swivel and churn, if you could
break your neck
        and be alive, head a lit house

sweeping its beam
        through the constructed real, I

tied you up—

inside my mind—

where you're sweating now, fisting under the bands—

Salt in your eye, can't lift a finger.

What use had I for hands.

Desire

So you can have a form—
So the definition's tacked down round your
        fleshy field:
Mine,

        Belovèd —

The gold shaft piercing the warm morass
        of the feminine feminine mind.

And when it recedes, after spilling its coins?
        When the new form fades, and leaves...

For a minute you were lit—
For a minute you knew what it's like to be bright,
        to be the sculpted, cherished thing—

You have a form: white fingers
        dragging at the shore,
the sea trying to crawl from its pit—

And above the sun shining, without hands.

Isolato

I snowed for years.

You swallowed hope, the crooked-fingered star —

The light never went out of my belly —

You snowed for years.

⌒

Sails, bunched in the harbor, blooming and contracting
    like a slovenly heart,
all seventeen in an unruly mass, some
    trying to pull away —

You wouldn't feel your loss —
    You made it art, the beautiful object, tears, waste
and the diamond in it, you said
    he left me, he left me, like geese on the fly
hands fat with ether —
    saw through your grief the boats on the lake and said

    the sails are white knives crossing over the water,
    they slice and re-slice the sky.

Clicking too shut jeweled Jewelry Box

with your How Sequined, How   Pre-Raphaelite

boats so much brighter on the water

than knives you imagined, white knives you imagined, not

lamp, sun, on the white of the sail

men unmooring their aluminum music

how bright quick sharp sun came they came
                    fast diamonds running on the blue-dark lake —

                         I snowed for years

in your spine there are boats —

                         I swallowed hope

a sail, to be lifted —

                         I sold it for a crown

to rush brightly in music —

                         I sold it for a barge

on the hand of one sailor —

                         Isolato with a crown

at the helm: Heart's Desire —

                         Isolato with a barge

the clay of you dumb at the rail at the prow,
    foraging for ornamental forms —

                    by Isolato, I am engorged.

Desire

A golden wedding in a golden mean, golden apples
      ripening
to sexual red, in their orderly, well-tended rows —

Apples, the divisive rewards for *Beauty*, in some fucked-up
      Greek-minded way —

But a darkness in there somewhere, right?
      Worm, snake, mealy texture that is the apple's spite —

      the sensual in us
offended —

not that the honey is withheld, but that it disappoints
      our *idea* of it —

so that pain is not in the lack, but rather in
      the having —

the reddest of all red apples abandoned —
      the skin broken, just a little, by the teeth.

Gift Drawing

Diamond of ocher day.

Diamond of violet night.

Squaring the cell
in which something was caged, something
    the color of a coffee stain—

Something.

A chosen blur.

For wasn't it
the center of the temple, cell
    in which the bride was trapped—

Friday night, still unbeloved.

Only Amish quilts, plate after plate
in your heavy
    book on art.

A little visual Valium. It might sedate
the churn of your restless eye—:

    thirty variations on *center-square*, always the opaque
diaphane, God
    you couldn't see through—

Then after a long while you turn the page.

And the marrow-colored cotton of the center-square
becomes a bone-field
squeezing out a tree —

stiff as wrought iron, green boughs curling into
humming fruits, a round
crop of suns —

in the *gift drawing*, from the nineteenth century's
spirit invasion:

harps, lamps, thimbles of light

you only half-believe —

fruits, flat as plates.
Buoying weightless
off the iron limbs —

until you see. The tree
doesn't throw any shadows, it spreads front and center
in relentless light —

Was that the gift? That *having*
was all at the surface: serum, persimmon, sweet
leaf —

Unbeloved. It couldn't darken

the ruthless eminence of things.

I Hunched Boiling Inside It

I was sweltering down the street, wondering why
when we lost limbs
it wasn't in a matter-of-fact, assembly-line way.

Why they weren't replaceable parts.

Thumb, bone, blood, the soul's
utilitaria—

Sheets of heat. Each pore stoppered
by a hot little grain of air—

The sun and I stewed in opposite corners.

Mine was called: Blood-pot.

It said, Pain is the ring.

By which the soul keeps its wedding vows.

Painting Vacation

At the card store she chose the pictogram for "clarity" over the pictogram
for "joy."

And the light said, Be mine.

And you said, Could you put a little yellow in it, could you make it
a little warmer —

And the light said, Lie down with the coats of the lovers who are
rising up out of a field full of poppies —

As she was explaining the difference between "honest" and "true," the Russian
student took her hand in his, saying, You don't have to be teacher, all the time.

You tried to draw sunlight on waves but it was elusive.

During the tarot reading she received "happiness" in the place of decision
and responsibility.

Beached shapes were easiest: sea-kelp down with its
string of black flies, raven picking through the drift —

Thinking about the card store: "happiness" was something to buy
    other people —

                not able to escape the feeling that it was trite —

                ⌒〜

then *strife*, with all its agitations — and *futility*, the certainty that forbids
all wealth —

Sometimes she was happy: the city in winter, under the cutting light,
    that she yearned for through all the heated bleedings of summer —

        The light saying, *Be mine.*
        You saying, *Tear the dark caul from the sea.*

Desire

For a minute prizes didn't matter because the black-and-white spider
      sat in the daisy.

Two ducks along the shore that the ice storm had ravaged,
      so that there were more blue lupine than before —

And in fact everything was more vivid because it had once suffered defeat:
      the rocks were blooming,
                  there were less places to sit —

For a long time the prize was a clear place to sit, inside of all that was
      resurging —

So that winning equaled the dust-blue tails of lupine?

When you had been thinking it was more like the man
      kayaking out there,
                  against the triangular wakes of the speedboats.

For a minute the prize was forgetting about it. For a minute the lake's
      silver page —

field that was mirroring creation —

that there was a clear place to sit,
                inside of all that wanting —

Sumer Is Icumen In

Larkspur at the gate like a wedding, the white, the purple-blue hue —

> *And when the woman with the oxygen tank walked by, you*
> *imagined a woman with an oxygen tank, a man so in love*
> *with her he imagines the slim tubes at each of her nostrils*
> *tendriling out and coiling right into his chest —*

red roses in the middle *if the heart could burst its blood out of joy inexpressible*
like a heart attack —

A hummingbird hovered in front of me and flashed its magenta breast.

JOY HOVERED IN FRONT OF ME AND FLASHED ITS MAGENTA BREAST

and was gone, that quick emblem,

> *and it was the single day giving you the poem,*
> *it was the kingdom saying, Come in —*

Because you were not chosen who would choose you

(you thought that kind of pain was adolescent, it wasn't
supposed to be present
in the present —)

> *so in love with you you want to breathe —*

the bluejay on the telephone wire turned its body so its head
was at its tail

making a *C*, incomplete circle, letting all the happiness out
or in—

Because you were not chosen who would choose you

(you thought since you were not chosen you shouldn't
let anyone choose—)

so in love with her he wants to breathe
for her —

but she would not even look at him;
wedded as she was to her incapacitation —

Because you were not chosen who would choose—

And X was on the cover of Y,
A and Z in each other's arms on every bench you passed—

Still the clouds were extraordinary today.
Still the roses decided to bloom all at once.
You carried your particular envy and perplexity everywhere
through the orange-scented air

and the day was not made less beautiful—:

the larkspur all bunched together at the gate,
their pastels milling around that
            red bride
as she opened her nine hearts,
            and you stood there thinking, Who
                    would choose me?
                            when the day had already chosen—

White Dog

Jingling,
> and the padding of feet, the sniffing
between the door and your floor—
> and they're in.
The dark one leaping up on the left, the white one
> jumping up on the right
as you lie asleep in your bed.
> But you're awake.
Can't get up now, dreamer.
> It's a delight the way they nose you,
wagging their black and white tails—
> until the dark one retreats.
Little pug with its saucer eyes, looking tremblingly
> at you—
and the white one suddenly cool. The white one
> lifting its leg—

Can't get up.
> The musk streams down.
And the white dog turns its moon head, looks steadily
> at you—
White light.
> White light.
Marking you, saying,
> You're mine.

Adept

Without a knife he opened himself up.

Without a knife.

Chinese letters marched around him in formation,
        a military equestrian parade —

He was an adept, in my book on the golden flower.

On a bed of peacock tails.

And he was opening his abdomen with both his hands,
        parting it like curtains.

And I thought if I looked at him long enough, I might go through there.

Through the flame-shaped opening.

Where there sat another lotus-sitting figure.

And the caption said, Origin of a new being in the place of power.

And I thought, Was that the flower.

What was the body but a scalpel and a light what was it —

Rubbing an oil into scars like a river for the first time I touched them —

I was an adept in the book of vivid pain, I used my finger like a knife —

Not
    to hurt myself, but to somehow get back *in* —

like the little man opening his belly right up,
        and the little man resting inside there.

But how could I. When I would not enter the flame-shaped opening.

When I hovered
                above.

Never leaving it, always nearing it, a fly on the verge of something
        sweet —

Was that what the body was, a sweetness?

Hive ringed by fire.

And the adept says, That's you on the bed: Empty Chamber.

And your stomach
                is open like a coat —

It's black in there, deep.
It's red in there, thick
                with the human loam —

And all along your ghost head and your shoulders
        you can feel the wet

as you slide back in,
       your tissues cupping you like hands.

The body: worm round an ember of light.

You're in it now.

Flower.

Notes

Techno:

"Serious killer" is part of a refrain to "Serial Thrilla," a song by the band Prodigy.

Quelquechose:

"The conflict between harmony and invention" is borrowed from the Vivaldi composition of the same name.

Suttee:

The main action takes place along the concrete banks of the Los Angeles River.

White Field:

Chamisa (or rabbitbrush) is a pungent flowering bush native to northern New Mexico.

The Washing:

The poem was sparked by a photo by Teun Voeten that accompanied "The Forensics of War," by Sebastian Junger (*Vanity Fair,* October 1999).

Working Methods:

The poem originally appeared in *The American Poetry Review*'s "In the Studio" series.

Ambivalent Light:

The quote that ends the first section is taken from *The Portrait of a Lady,* by Henry James.

Isolato:

Many thanks to Larissa Szporluk for the persistence of the title.

Gift Drawing:

"Gift drawings" were visual records of messages Shaker women
received from heavenly spirits during the Era of Manifestations, a
period of intense religious zeal among Shakers in the mid-1800s.

Adept:

The poem was sparked by an illustration in *The Secret of the Golden
Flower*, attributed to Lü Yen, eighth century. Translated from the
Chinese by Richard Wilhelm (1931), with commentary by C.G. Jung.

About the Author

Dana Levin grew up in Lancaster, California, and graduated from Pitzer College and the Graduate Creative Writing Program at New York University. Her first book, *In the Surgical Theatre*, won the 1999 American Poetry Review/Honickman First Book Prize. It went on to receive many honors, including the 2000 Witter Bynner Prize from the American Academy of Arts and Letters, the 2000 GLCA New Writers Award, the 2000 John C. Zacharis First Book Award from *Ploughshares*, and the 2003 PEN/Osterweil Award. Her work has appeared in the anthologies *American Poetry: The Next Generation* (Carnegie Mellon University Press, 2000), *My Business Is Circumference: Poets on Influence and Mastery* (Paul Dry Books, 2001), *The Poet's Child* (Copper Canyon Press, 2002), and *This Art: Poems about Poetry* (Copper Canyon Press, 2003), as well as in many magazines. She is the recipient of three Pushcart Prizes, a 1999 National Endowment for the Arts fellowship, a 2001 Lannan Residency fellowship, the 2003 Robert Frost Fellowship in Poetry from the Breadloaf Writers' Conference, a 2004 Witter Bynner Fellowship from the Library of Congress, and a 2004 Writer's Award from the Rona Jaffe Foundation. Levin teaches in the MFA program at Warren Wilson College and directs the Creative Writing Program at the College of Santa Fe.

The Chinese character for poetry is made up of two parts: "word" and "temple." It also serves as pressmark for Copper Canyon Press. Founded in 1972, Copper Canyon Press remains dedicated to publishing poetry exclusively, from Nobel laureates to new and emerging authors. The Press thrives with the generous patronage of readers, writers, booksellers, librarians, teachers, students, and funders—everyone who shares the conviction that poetry invigorates the language and sharpens our appreciation of the world.

Major funding has been provided by:

The Paul G. Allen Family Foundation

Lannan Foundation

National Endowment for the Arts

The Starbucks Foundation

Washington State Arts Commission

For information and catalogs:

COPPER CANYON PRESS
Post Office Box 271
Port Townsend, Washington 98368
360-385-4925
www.coppercanyonpress.org

Wedding Day is set in the font Filosofia, Zuzana Licko's contemporary interpretation of the work of Giambattista Bodoni. Book design and composition by Valerie Brewster, Scribe Typography. Printed on archival-quality Glatfelter Author's Text at McNaughton & Gunn, Inc.